SPARKS
FROM MY EMBERS

Missionary Poems
by Arlene Updyke

Published by Baptist Mid-Missions
Cleveland, Ohio

SPARKS FROM MY EMBERS

Copyright 2000 by Arlene Updyke

Unless otherwise indicated, Scripture quotations in this book are taken from the Holy Bible, King James Version, 1611

Library of Congress Control Number: 00-093447
   Updyke, Arlene A., 1929-
   Sparks From My Embers: Missionary Poems by Arlene Updyke

ISBN No. 0-941645-04-5

Published by Baptist Mid-Missions
P.O. Box 308011
Cleveland, OH 44130-8011

Credits:
Copyright 2000 Olan Mills Photography
Author's photograph used by permission Olan Mills Photography

Copyright 1994-1997 Broderbund Home Division of The Learning Company
Permission granted by Broderbund for use of computer graphics.

Cover design and graphics layout by Jurell Powell McCrorie

To order, send $9.95 + $2.00 S. & H. per copy to
Sparks From My Embers
2318 So. Hosmer St.
Tacoma, WA 98405
aupdyke@compuserve.com

Printed in the United States of America by Bentson Printing Co., Tacoma, Washington 98402

DEDICATION

To Ken, my beloved husband, whose unfailing patience
freed me to write.

To Amy, Elizabeth and Bruce, my children, who gave me love and laughter and song in the hard times.

To Bud Cairns, a dear friend and one of my very first encouragers.

To Elsie Bartlett, a precious friend who, when desperately ill, urged me to publish.

FORWARD

As a child growing up in El Paso, Texas, I thought some of being a missionary although I was not a Christian. My family moved up to Washington State at the outbreak of World War II. At fourteen, I heard for the first time how Jesus Christ died for my sin, and I turned my life over to Him. When I was sixteen, God called me to be a missionary. I had no idea where I would go or when, but following high school, I began training as a nurse in Tacoma, Washington, intending to go to Africa as a missionary nurse. There I attended the Temple Baptist Church and learned of Baptist Bible Seminary (BBS) in Johnson City, New York. Believing God wanted me there to prepare for missionary service, I left Washington following graduation as a registered nurse.

In my first year at BBS, I met a third-year student, Ken Updyke, who also wanted to go to Africa He became interested in a certain nurse who could go with him and "put *Band-Aids* on his owies" on the mission field. We fell in love and were married in 1953. One year later Baptist Mid-Missions accepted us as missionary appointees - destination Ghana, West Africa in 1955. Our four-month old baby went with us. We bought a one-way ticket.

For our first assignment we made a bumpy two-day trip on red washboard roads to the large village of Wa in the Ghana hinterland. We spent two terms there and had two more babies. Our ministries included working in language, village evangelism and nursing experience in a small clinic. The first term was shortened due to plans to return and open a medical clinic in a remote village. Beth, our second baby, had developed heart problems and needed evaluation in the States. We returned to Ghana, after a year of furlough with Beth completely well.

During our second term in Wa, plans for the clinic failed because of government restrictions. We turned to other ministries including language learning, planting churches in villages, writing an initial grammar for the Waalii language and acting as the first house parents in the children's home for the little school we organized in 1963. Ken also taught in the newly organized Wa Bible Institute, I had two miscarriages in Wa and another during our second furlough.

The village of Tumu needed a missionary replacement. We transferred there where we spent eight years. Tumu was a hard place, a testing ground for trust in trial. Many of the poems were written there. We worked in camp ministry, government schools, organized the Lilexi Baptist Church and developed a youth program with a rank system similar to AWANA here in the States. Separated from our children for the first time, we experienced that grief. I had another miscarriage and our family stopped with the precious three God had already given to us. But in Tumu, we drew closer to the God of all comfort and learned to lean hard. I also operated a "veranda clinic", helping women who came by with their babies for medical treatment. A different language challenged our desire to break the language barrier. We translated and printed a couple of simple Bible storybooks in the local Sissala dialect. Our first experience in printing primers in the Waalii language also came at this time.

Meanwhile, our children were in boarding schools in Ghana and the Ivory Coast (for high school). We missed them desperately but committed them to the One Who loved them even more than we. At the end of our second term in Tumu, we were asked to transfer to the capital city following our furlough. There we spent ten years interrupted by trips back to the States for medical furloughs emergency intervention with one of our children and a wedding. In Accra, our ministries multiplied. Involved in church planting, interim pastoring, and printing, we saw the years speed past until our health dictated our permanent return home. Both of us had surgeries, Ken undergoing his first cardiac bypass operation. We said good-bye to Ghana after more than twenty seven years of serving the King there.

In 1984, we moved to Tacoma, Washington to plant an inner-city church. Organized in 1985, Beacon Baptist Church now owns its buildings and is growing under godly leadership. We retired from that ministry and to serve senior saints in nearby Temple Baptist Church. As long as God gives us strength, we hope to continue to serve Him with gladness. He is worthy!

We could recount *many* adventures with God both in Ghana and in America. But in the good times and bad, we found Him faithful, loving and kind. "Oh, the men would praise the Lord for His goodness and for His wonderful works to the children of men." Psalm 107:8

Table of Contents

Surrender

I wrote this after graduating from Tacoma General Hospital School of Nursing in 1950. I lived in a rooming house with two other girls, and we cooked our own meals. A dear friend, Beth, helped me to remain close to God, continually reminding me of the need for Quiet Times spent with Him alone. I worked a year and then went off to Baptist Bible Seminary to prepare for missionary service.

Take Me

Take this vessel, O my God,
Poor and empty though it be;
Fill it with a godly filling;
Let Thy glory shine through me.

Take the lost and wasted moments.
Lord, how many now have gone!
Give me hours of blessed service
Spent for Thee, the Holy One.

Take the words I should have spoken,
Words of life to other hearts;
Give my mouth a heav'nly message
Which the Holy Ghost imparts.

Take my heart so cold and selfish,
Thinking only of its own;
Give it, Lord, a warm compassion,
Thinking of its King alone.

Thou art still my God on High,
Glorious, worthy to be praised;
Grant me life on higher ground
Through Him Who from death was raised.

Father, Son, and Holy Spirit,
Three in One, I need Thee all,
Helping me to live victorious,
Working, waiting for Your call.

Six months after we met, Ken asked me to go steady with him - a very big event in college life. I joyfully accepted his ring, putting layers and layers of tape around it to make it fit. Then, I stopped to think that we had not prayed much about this very important decision which would most likely lead to marriage. I didn't want to make a tragic mistake. So I gave the ring back to him and suggested that we spend time in prayer to make absolutely sure this was the right move. He agreed to take back the ring, though he himself had no doubts. I went back to the dorm brokenhearted, because I loved him so. I was afraid he would change his mind. Later, I received the ring and wore it gladly. That happened in 1952 and the love remains. I review this poem whenever I meet a test of God's will which wrings my heart.

Thy Will

Can I count Thy will as sweet when it tears this heart of mine?

Can I kneel at Thy dear feet seeking, not my way, but Thine?

Only through the strength of Christ I can such decisions make,

When it seems as though my heart with this struggle fierce should break!

When Ken and I were attending Baptist Bible Seminary in 1952, Ken became discouraged, with working and taking a full load of classes, including Greek, third-year English Composition and Systematic Theology, in addition to other less difficult subjects. He was so downhearted that he almost felt he could not continue to carry this load. But he knew that God wanted him in Africa as a missionary. In trying to encourage him, I wrote this poem. It was one of the first of the many I wrote to him through the years.

He Knows the Way I Take - Job 23:8-12

Oh, take, my God, these hands that tremble at my side;
Thou knowest, Lord God, that I would close to Thee abide.
Almighty Father, hear my plea break from my lips.
Oh, take my fearful heart, and all that fear eclipse!
My Lord (for Thou art mine), the way before me lies;
I grope into its mist in search of Paradise.
Alas! that ghost Despair would drive me from my goal.
I know not what to do. Lord, calm my weary soul.
Yea, I have heard Thy call and followed its clear ring,
And yet - the way seems dim; alone to Thee I cling.
My glorious Savior, now bestow on me release,
And grant that in Thy trust my soul shall find Thy peace.
I cannot see the way nor know what lies before,
But I can lean on Thee, the One whom I adore.
My Master, Lord o'er all, the Rose of Sharon sweet,
I take Thy sovereign will and rest - at Thy blest feet.

In my first year at Bible College, I read about Christian martyrs and sat down to have a serious discussion with my heart. How could I ever endure some of the tortures that were a part of various persecutions in history? Maybe I should reconsider my faith and go back on it. But thinking about it convinced me that this could never be. Christ was so much a part of my heart that life without Him was inconceivable. So I counted the cost and wrote this poem.

Maybe

Maybe tomorrow will find us
Facing a martyr's grave.
Then shall we praise with joy anew
His mighty power to save.

How could I face such conflict?
Whence should my strength arise?
Up to my blessed Master
I gaze with tear-dimmed eyes.

"Lord, would I were courageous,
That I could bravely die;
Forbid me the shame of a coward,
Strangle my weakling cry!

Yea, Lord, come upon me with power
And grant, that if that day should come,
I'll joyfully praise my Redeemer
And welcome the way He leads Home!

But wait - give me power to live, Lord,
As fearlessly as I would die;
Be with me each day as my Captain
The whole host of Hell to defy".

One of our chapel speakers spoke of our hearts being soft enough to bear the image of Christ on them, much as sealing wax receives the imprint of the signet ring and carries the symbol of the one sending an important message. The importance of the wax is directly linked to the signet ring. So our most important task is to live our lives for Jesus Christ in order that others will know we belong to Him. At the time I wrote this, Ken and I were engaged, and I wanted the first place in my heart to belong to Jesus.

Molded By Him

Father, keep me soft as wax,
Molded to Thy will.
Oh! I would not hardened be;
Help me Self to kill!

All must be laid at Thy feet,
Yielded to Thy touch.
Let me give into Thy hands
The things I love so much.

In my life, first place must be
Given to Thy Son.
Melt me, blessed God, I pray.
Vict'ry must be won!

On our return to Ghana for our third term we transferred to the village of Tumu in the far north country. A border village, it had a fair amount of traffic going and coming from the country of Burkino Fasso, then known as Upper Volta. This little land locked country was poorer than Ghana, but sometimes we found foodstuffs there unavailable in Ghana, especially during times of governmental unrest such as coups and counter coups. The villagers, mostly farmers, scraped a *hardscrabble* existence from the hard dry soil with short - handled hoes and no plows. Some called it The Hunger Village. I thought of it as the end of the road. We lived in Tumu for eight years, in six and one-half of which we worked without missionary co-workers. At the time, we could not see the benefits of this. We came to know the nationals well and learned how to communicate with them in their language. I had a medical ministry from my "veranda clinic" where I dispensed medicine to the women as they passed by the house on their way to market, their sick babies tied securely to their backs. The small government clinic in town opened for business only a few hours a day. So our house became sort of a walk-in clinic. (When we left for furlough, one man said to me, "Who will take care of our children now?")

We sorely missed our children away in boarding schools. The sun beat down on the baked earth in the long dry season. Sharing the diseases of the people - malaria, eye infections, *river blindness* - we thus identified with them. But the oppressive heat, the relentless winds blowing down from the Sahara for three months, the shortage of fresh foods and eggs, loneliness, and primarily, the absence of the children made me long for the States more than once. Yes, I almost wanted to quit. But God strengthened my heart, as He always does when we seek Him for comfort and find refuge in His Word, the Bible. We stayed, we learned, we endured and finished our course with joy.

20

Bind the Sacrifice - Psalm 118:27

It matters not what Thou hast planned for others, Lord of
mine,
A way of life enclosed by friends, of ease and comfort too,
Security, companionship, close fellowship with saints;
When Thou hast marked a path for me apart from children
dear -
Of anxious hours with loved ones ill, and loneliness and
heat.
It matters not - Lord, hear my cry and bind the sacrifice
Securely to the altar where it once lay passive there.
Prevent these eyes from looking back, the hand ta'en from
the plow;
Thine, Thy disciple would I be where'er Thou sendest me.
Now give me rest 'mid pressures here, and peace within
the storm,
And ah! let me consider Him and passive lie once more
Beneath Thy hand and take therefrom whate'er Thou givest
me -
A sacrifice acceptable and holy for my God.

One Valentine's Day in Ghana, at a weekly station meeting with fellow missionaries, I felt a poem "coming on." So I scribbled this off while others were talking and then read it to them as a part of the devotional time we always had.

Give Me Your Heart

Give Me your heart; I will change it, will mend it,
and then rearrange it.
I'll sweep out the darkness, the gloom and the sin,
The fears and the selfishness lying within.
I'll clean it and leave it as neat as a pin
If you'll only allow Me to change it.

A new heart I'll put in its place; the difference will
show on your face.
Where once there was discord and anger and
fear,
There now will be singing and praises and cheer.
Your friends will all wonder, when once it is clear
That your heart has been changed by My grace.

What's this? You're afraid of some loss? Not
ready to take up the cross?
Your will is held back, to your weakness you cling;
You're afraid that somehow only suffering I'll bring,
So you grasp every tarnished and worrisome thing,
Rejecting the gold for the dross.

Oh! My child! Put your heart in My hand.
Trust in Me though you don't understand!
When you once taste the joy of surrender in life
And place your heart willingly under My knife,
Say good-bye to the pride and the fears and the
strife -
You will enter God's Love and Peace Land.

On my various furloughs away from the field, I wrote poems as the mood struck me. This was on of those times, when I asked myself the important questions of: Who will listen? Who will follow? Who will worship? My prayer came at the end.

Who?

Who will follow after Him,
Letting not His call grow dim,
Yielding not to any whim,
Will you?

Who will listen for His call,
Yield and follow, leaving all,
Caring not whate'er befall,
Will I?

Who will kneel before His feet
Counting tribulation sweet,
Only longing Him to meet,
Shall we?

Lord, my heart You now do see;
May it tender, yielded be,
Giving all it loves to Thee,
I pray.

Trials & Testing

1951 - my first year at Bible College! Wanting His will, I sought His guidance for a missionary career and place to serve, His choice of a mate for me, the length of my course of study, and where to work and live. I prayed this prayer.

Let Thy Promise Be My Refuge

Father, how I need Thee now. Keep my heart today
Overflowing with Thy love, this alone I pray.
Only through Thy blessed peace can my heart be still.
Keep me looking unto Thee, waiting for Thy will.
I have leaned upon Thine arm, have Thy guidance sought;
Keep me broken, bended, low, living as I ought,
So that when the future dawns, it may find me still
Glorifying Thy dear Son, living in Thy will.

One furlough, a curious woman asked if I had experienced fear. "Oh, yes!" I replied, "Many times!" I don't know if a missionary woman can be immune to fear. I was not. But the Bible comforted me. If human beings were not a prey to fear, there would not be so many verses in the Bible telling us not to fear! More than once, I feared that one of our children might not survive a deadly illness; feared for the snakes and scorpions around (and sometimes in) the house; feared when diseases such as meningitis and hepatitis were present in epidemic proportions. I was afraid of rabid dogs that came into our yard (one biting our dog and causing the death of a loved puppy). I fought fear in coups, revolutions, and unrest. But God, the sovereign, eternal God, calmed my heart and gave me this poem in Tumu.

Fear

Fear! Whirling, swirling round me like a blizzard of despair
-
A whirlpool, pulling me inexorably to the deadly vortex of destruction.
I cry from the storm, "Lord! Help!"
From the black pool, "Jehovah! Save!"
Who can find his way in blinding storm,
Or escape the wall of the maelstrom? None.

Am I helpless? At the mercy of the evil?
Ah no!

There is One Who promises to save His very own;
His outstretched arm of righteousness will reach within the storm,
And draw me out exhausted, but safe and sane with Him.
His mighty hand the deadly pool cannot resist. It yields
My feeble, weakened frame unto the One Who rescues me.

Dear Lord! Keep me so close to Thee that fear cannot destroy
My peace and joy and hope in Thee, my rest beneath Thy wings.
I will not lose my confidence in whirlpool or fierce storm;
The Lord's my refuge and my GOD, and Him alone I'll trust.

So often in Tumu my strength ebbed. By the fourth year in that Subsahara heat, I felt that I was just 'marking time' without accomplishing very much. Psalm 18:1 and 2, brought me great comfort and support. "I will love Thee, O LORD, my strength. The LORD is my rock, and my fortress, and my deliverer; my God, my strength, in whom I will trust; my buckler and the horn of my salvation and my high tower." I leaned and learned.

From My Weak Heart

When I am ready to drop on the way,
King of my life, Sun of my soul;
Ready to fall 'neath Despair's heavy blow -
Lord, keep me under control!

Keep me, Lord, steady to walk on ahead,
Facing the storm, grasping Thy hand;
Nor flinching, nor shrinking from God-given task,
Eager to do Thy command.

Show me the giants to be what they are -
Tools of the wicked; evil at bay;
Give me the grace then to stand up and fight,
Lord, keep me strong on the way!

One of the lady missionaries, in Ghana longer than I, wrote to me expressing her extreme fatigue and frustration with not being able to do all that she wanted to do for God. I wrote this for Artus Larkin, but my years in Tumu echoed in my mind. "Dear Lord, I'm SO tired! I'm not really accomplishing much for You. Give me Your strength." So He tests us, tries us, proves us. Psalm 66:10 says, "For You, O God, have proved us. You have tried us as silver is tried."

Into the Crucible

Into the crucible, tested by fire,
God poured my spirit to suffer and burn;
There in the agony, fainting and heartsore,
I cried to Him for relief from distress.

"Father, so weak am I, bearing this testing;
Gone is my strength 'til I see it no more;
How can I run the race when I am slow, Lord?
Weary and weakened, I plead for Thy help."

Softly He spoke to me, "Within this crucible
I shall yet try thee to come forth as gold;
Trust in the Goldsmith to fashion a beautiful
Object to glorify Jesus alone."

So I allow Him to do as He willeth,
Silently under His hand I will trust;
He's my sufficiency. What matters weakness?
God is my help! I shall come forth as gold!

Sometimes a missionary must leave early for medical furlough and no one takes his place. Another cannot return for medical or family reasons. Recruits are not coming fast enough to replace those who retire or cannot return. What do the remaining missionaries do? They roll up their sleeves a little higher and try to pick up the slack as much as possible - and cry to God, "Lord of the harvest, send forth reapers!"

A Missionary's Lament

Spread yourself a little thinner,
Choose another task or two;
Work until your heart is weary -
For the laborers are few.

Weep because your strength is failing,
Try a few more things to do;
Keep on pushing, keep on plugging -
For the laborers are few.

Mourn because a work goes downward
With no shepherd yet in view;
Cry to God for wand'ring members,
For the laborers are few.

Lord of Harvest, send forth reapers,
Gather up our strength anew.
Give Thy call for reinforcements -
LORD! The laborers are few!

Worship

I worked for a year after nurse's training to earn tuition for college. This gave adequate time to think, prepare my heart and consider my future as a missionary. As I looked inside and saw the frailties, the self-interest, the wrong motives, I sought Him and realized that my Savior wanted so much more from me than I was giving Him.

A Broken Heart

The Man of Sorrows, looking down from Glory, now I see;
His heart is wounded, deeply hurt for what He finds in me.
Oh! worthless bit of clay am I, that for the sake of self
Would seek to lay aside His grace and set it on a shelf.
On no! not grace for me, for that I gladly do receive,
But love and grace for others and the things they should
believe.
How CAN they know except they're taught, and that just
through the Word?
And if I fail to show the Way, how CAN they know my
Lord?
Oh, Master, break my heart today and make it truly Thine.
Just cast out all the selfishness - yea, make my life to
shine;
That Thou, when Thou dost look again, Thy heart will joyful
be
Because I have deserted self, to follow only Thee.

On my twenty-second birthday, a dear friend, Beth, gave me a book written by the Puritan theologian, John Owen. Its title, *The Glory of Christ,* and contents inspired this poem.

Seek His Glory

Seek ye His glory, ye His children bought
And ransomed by His blood so freely shed;
Can ye not see your Master as He stands
And pleads with God the Father in your stead?
The wide expanse of sky He sprayed with stars,
He bade them shine to give our souls delight;
From that fair realm He bowed Himself so low
To give a world of blackness its one Light.
So great the host of angels that adore
The Son of God in all His majesty.
That they unnumbered are - yet we who know
His grace, do not cry out in ecstasy.
E'en when He trod the earth in servant's form,
His Godhead and His glory still were shown;
Transfigured on the Mount, Gethsemane -
Disciples witnessed Deity alone.
If we will give the glory due His name,
Much sweeter still our daily walk will grow,
And we will find, that as we look to Him,
Our lives from glory unto glory will go.

GLORY

Oh, the joys of studying in a Christian college where fellow students seek and find some of the riches of the character of God and the Bible. They grow together in knowledge and friendship. Some fall in love and find their life mates. Most graduate with the knowledge of what they want to do with their lives. Ken and I met and married while we both were still in school. But the most important thing I gained in those three years was a new love of Jesus Christ. Ken said to me when he asked me to marry him, "I want you to know that Jesus will always be first in my life." That suited me just fine!

The One, The Only

One burning thought - My Savior;
One heartfelt joy - My Lord.
One tender voice - My Shepherd,
One message sweet - The Word.
One highest prayer - My Master;
One resting place - My Rock.
One blessed Hope - He's coming,
And I - one in His flock!

In Bible College, one struggles with discovering exact meaning for some words learned in Theology class. The study of God, His nature and His attributes, stretches the mind. I wrote this to give to myself a definition of four of these.

Mercy, Love, Grace, and Peace

MERCY- what is mercy?
When foolish doubts crowd in my mind;
To His blessed will my eyes seem blind;
Yet through it all His love I find!
This is mercy.

THE LOVE OF GOD - what is it?
When filthy with the shame of sin;
When helpless, as I've always been,
He comes, my heart to dwell within -
This is God's own love.

GRACE - what is grace?
A heart unworthy as is mine
Is taken, Father, to be Thine,
And Thou dost work to make it shine--
This is grace.

PEACE - what is peace?
The molehills grow to mountains steep;
He bids me rest, for He doth keep;
And then may I lie down and sleep.
And this is His blessed peace!

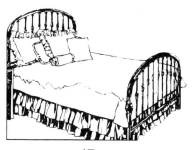

In the Fall of 1952, as a young woman in her second year at college, I struggled with many emotions, problems of disciplining my life to study and work, and neglect of my quiet times with Him. He hears the cries of His children and ministered to my hurting heart.

Lord of Glory, Mighty Counselor

<u>Alas!</u>

"Watch and pray that ye enter not into temptation
for the spirit indeed is willing, but the flesh is weak."
Matthew 26.41

Alas, O Lord, I cannot look upon my life today,
For there my heart uncovered lies with many thoughts of sin;
And when I realize that love that Thou has proferred me,
I cry aloud, "Oh, thank you, Lord for all of mighty grace!"
The Lord of glory, Prince of Peace, the Mighty Counselor
Has chosen this poor life of mine to serve and follow Him.
O, Savior dear! I bend my life today to Thy blessed will;
My heart is overflowing with Thy great sufficiency.
In me I can do nothing, but in Thee I can do all.
Oh, happy is the life with Thee when Thou art King and Lord!

Prince of Peace

One furlough year as I lay in bed, trying to get to sleep, these words came to my mind.

What Will It Be?

I lay on my bed in the darkness,
When sleep would not come with its balm;
My thoughts, they were centered on Jesus;
He brought to my heart peace and calm.

I pondered, "When ends all my toil,
what will it be like to be there -
To lift up my eyes to the wonder
of seeing Him glorified, fair?

Ah! surely the sight will o'erwhelm me,
His face bright and radiant with love;
"Am I really here?" I will question,
"Have angel hosts borne me above?"

To think - nevermore to be tired,
Never a sorrow or pain;
Never a fear or a worry,
Never a teardrop again.

Always - sweet joy and a chorus of praises
to Him on the throne;
Always a sense of deep gladness
He chose me as one of His own.

For years I have followed His footprints
through valleys and hills, dark and light;
In weariness often, and weeping,
still always by faith and not sight.

But now - let me see my Beloved;
let me gaze on His beautiful face;
Let me bow at His feet, scarred and nail-pierced,
and adore Him for blood-purchased grace.

I can nevermore grieve Him with fretting,
nevermore fight against sin;
Walking with Jesus in glory,
filled with peace both without and within.

Then I dropped off to sleep,
ever smiling to think of the joys still ahead;
My heart was in Heav'n with my Savior,
my body still captive in bed.

But soon comes release,
and the rapture of being for aye at His side;
I'll gaze on the face of my Bridegroom and there,
loving Him, I'll abide.

prayer

Toward the end of our missionary career in Ghana where we spent twenty seven plus years, I became physically spent. Daily I asked the Lord for strength to get me through. One Sunday morning as I prepared for the services, my back ached, tropical heat poured through the window and I just wanted to stay home from church. Then I realized that I had a place of peace to resort to, right there by the kitchen counter. Often since then, I flee to my secret place and find the solace I need.

My Secret Place

There's a place where I withdraw from the worries of the
world,
Where I creep into my Savior's loving arms.
Outwardly I still can work, outwardly I seem unchanged,
But my spirit nestles there away from harms.

No one knows that I am there, save my Savior who will give
All the comfort that my weary spirit craves;
And I learn there to endure pain and loneliness and fear -
All of this I have, because my Jesus saves.

Ah! the blessedness to know of this secret place of rest!
I can go there day or night, at any hour;
All my troubled heart is still, all my cares are laid aside,
In that secret place I draw from Him new power.

I can face the world each day without pills or sedatives,
He controls my fears, my weakness is made strong;
And He gives me blessed peace, quiet heart, and patient
tongue,
Dries my tears and sends me onward with a song.

In lands where missionaries serve, no one can overestimate the value of those back home who are faithful in praying for the work, the workers and the blessing of God upon their endeavors. Many times when we felt ourselves sinking, we remembered the faithful ones who prayed for us. It helped to keep us there for twenty-seven years. Once when I wrote a distressed letter to two older prayer warriors, they replied, "We're praying for you, and we know that you will make it through this hard time."

Someone Is Kneeling to Pray

Again and again He has lifted our hearts
In the burden and heat of the day;
Our faith, it increases, anxiety ceases,
As someone is kneeling to pray.

Cast down but not out, facing battles so grim
We tremble to see the hard way;
But Jesus still lifts with blessings and gifts
For someone is kneeling to pray.

Be strengthened, my heart, God is sovereign still.
'Tis your place not to flee but to stay;
Your King's on the throne, He remembers His own
And someone is kneeling to pray.

After our retirement from the Ghana field, we began an inner-city ministry. Our strength was limited, our experience minimal. We encountered problems different from those prominent in the African bush. Here we had no famines, no tropical diseases, no language barrier. But we learned to extend love and compassion to those with abysmal family histories, those with limited opportunities because of their cultural orientation. Loving them was the easy part. Trying to help them made us realize we needed aid both from God Who knows all hearts and others who were more acquainted with the problems of the inner-city. The aid came from core workers, seminary students, and local pastors.

God Give Us Strength - 1986

God give us strength!
To battle wrong,
To sing Faith's song,
To lift the shining lamp of life aloft.

God give us strength!
To conquer doubt,
To shout Faith's shout,
Oh God, do not allow us to be soft!

God give us strength!
Our hands are weak,
The task too great,
We dare not stumble least we drop or fall.

God give us strength!
Our own is gone,
HIS is enough!
In that then, let us conquer, standing tall!

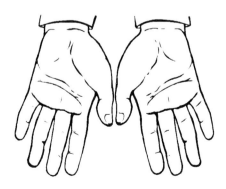

Call/Ministry

Before Ken asked me to marry him, he delivered a challenge to me. Could I really 'take it' in Africa? Didn't I know that difficulties and diseases awaited us if we went? He wanted to be sure that I weighed the risks before accepting his proposal. I sent him this answer.

A Challenge--1952

A challenge you have sent to me, Oh, friend of mine, the
one I love,
And how shall I best answer you?   For that, my soul must
look above.
God give me love to match his love, a happy heart to
cheer his own,
God grant that I may go with him where each would go for
Thee alone.
Dear Lord, I need the quiet strength to meet the stress of
every day;
God give us hearts that love Thy Word, that we should
read and pray.

Dear friend, you ask if I could bear to go to Africa with
you,
When living there is very hard - Ah yes, I know, all this is
true.
Do not forget that we are called to service in that blighted
land,
And if, in God's most perfect will, you come and take me
by the hand
To minister with you to those who need assurance of His
care,
Then 'twill be sweeter far to be in Africa than anywhere!

A challenge you have sent to me; I take it with a
trembling heart,
But know that if He leads the way, abundant joy He will
impart.

One furlough, on a golden summer evening, Ken sat at the table composing a sermon for an upcoming meeting. The mellow climate, the gorgeous scenery, the siren call to drop responsibility and go outside to play triggered these words.

My Master's Vineyard

Let others play and laugh in the sun,
They have their fill of frolic and fun,
But for me there's a task already begun -
'Tis work in the Master's vineyard.

The crowd calls out, "Come join in play,
Eat, drink, and laugh while still you may."
For me, my joy is but to stay
At work in the Master's vineyard.

The lights are bright, the music fast,
(That song shall turn to sob at last);
I look up to see the crowd sweep past
As I work in the Master's vineyard.

Let me not turn back, O Christ, from the way
Thou hast set before me; let me stay
Content to the ending of life's day
At work--in my Master's vineyard.

Not all of our missionary families come to the field intact and leave without loss of health, a mate, a child. Lives have been lost through road accidents and diseases. Some left the field broken in health or so damaged emotionally they could not return. Each must face the possibility of unforeseen losses. Each must count himself or herself as expendable for the sake of the One Who sent them. Only then will they remain to serve.

Few There Be Who Find It

Few there be who find the way that leads them into life;
Fewer far who take the path where fear and trials are rife.
The father lifts his face to God, in courage takes this way,
And mother gathers children 'round, so close to her they
stay.
Together, father, mother, bairns, they walk the altar road
Where living sacrifices tread. Ah! heavy seems the load!
"Oh God! Can we our little ones upon the altar lay,
Leave all our loved ones, kindred dear?"
They seem to hear Him say,
"I call you not to doubt and dread, nor to an awesome
fear;
So precious is your gift to me - I hold your children dear.
But in the heat of sacrifice pure gold I will bring forth;
The dross burned out, the offering will one day prove its
worth.
Before you lies a nation where I yet will people call;
And if you see but rough and steep a path, still give your
all.
And I will firmly grasp your hand, I'll lead the way for you.
I'll give you joy if you will trust your Lord to see you
through.
When others warn, stay close to Me - yea, close enough
to hear
Your Master's whisper, 'Fear thou not, for I am always
near.
Near enough to give you grace no matter what befall;
Near enough to give you joy as you obey My call.' "

Tumu, our border village, held delights as well as trials. One furlough, as I spoke to many women's groups in Washington State, we used the honoraria to buy a 50cc Honda motorcycle - efficient and small enough for each of the children and me to ride. We rode many miles on it before we sold it in preparation for going home at the end of the term. Naturally, riding it did not come easy for me! Once I drove right off the veranda because I didn't know how to use the hand brake. Another time, I rode into the water in the dam spillway. Some helpful men pushed it up the hill leading to the house, water spilling out the tailpipe as we went, Fortunately, it survived - and so did I! In time, we could laugh over these incidents. What a blessing that Honda was!

Over Yondah with My Honda

I was sent to work out yondah with my 50cc Honda
And I use it now for visits and for market.
It is surely no presumption that the gasoline consumption
Is the cheapest, and it's easy too to park it.

If the ladies from Seattle could observe me in the saddle
I am sure that they would just sit back and wondah;
For I dodge the goats and biddies, the lorries, and the kiddies
As I drive my Japanese-efficient Honda.

And my friends from old Tacoma ought to see me as I roam around
The village for my sick calls and my classes;
I return across the dam with bananas and a yam,
While the water gnats, they bump against my glasses.

Here's to all my friends (the best!) in the Evergreen Northwest
Who contributed the dollars for this wondah;
God will bless them, this I know, helping missionaries go
Over all the world to preach the Word by Honda.

In 1981, just before our last term in Ghana, we sailed away from Brooklyn harbor, leaving our three children behind. The oldest daughter was married. The second said good-bye with bitter tears, and the youngest, our only son, was off to college. I can still see the Statue of Liberty, green in the distance, a symbol of our nation and the dear ones we were leaving behind Standing by the rail, I quietly cried for missing them. I wrote when we arrived, "Now we are irrevocably committed to another term in Africa. Friends and loved ones are left behind. All the yearning of our hearts cannot bring them to our side. So our task, when we have weeping hearts, is to put on a brave front and keep shining for Him."

Led Away

Led away to suffer with You,
Led away from those we cherish,
Led to Ghana, there to serve You,
Led away to those who perish.

Led from Amy, Steve, and babies,
Beth and Bruce and those they care for;
Led from ease to daily struggle,
Led to love the ones we're there for.

Lamb of God, help me with parting!
Give me strength of heart to bear it;
Help me find afresh Your altar -
Know Your love and go to share it.

On our return to the States, I did some serious inventory, aware of my mortality.

The Road Ahead
Written at age 53

I'm walking the path of the older,
This is no time to hide or deny
The grim fact that youth is behind me
And life is so fast slipping by!
Let me gaze up ahead with clear thinking
And decide, even now, what my course
Of action would be could I choose it,
Ending life sans regret or remorse.

After almost twelve years, Beacon Baptist
Church, planted in Tacoma's inner city, graduated
from mission status and became independent.

Beacon Baptist Chruch after Ten Years
(For Pastor James and Sister Betty Bell)

Ten years ago we linked arms together
To serve the Lord in all kinds of weather.
We used our hands to welcome people,
Even though we had no steeple.
Worked and worked 'til the light of the moon,
Showed up at church with a wooden spoon.
We used our knees to bow in prayer
For those who needed His loving care.
Used our arms to give them hugs
And cried for those enslaved by drugs.
Used our ears to hear their woes,
Gave them food and passed out clothes.
With our eyes we saw the sorrow
Of those without a bright tomorrow.
Used our knuckles to knock on doors
As enlistees in the *Prince of Peace Corps*;
Used our feet to walk up and down
The streets in this old part of town.
We've laughed with them, cried with them,
Grieved with them, sighed with them,
Tried every way to get alongside of them.
But we had the answer to everyone's need -
The Lord Jesus Christ - for them He did bleed.
We taught them the Bible, God's holy Word,
And how to use skillfully this mighty sword.
So we have worked with you ten years together;
Thank God He brought us through rain and shine weather!

The years since our wedding day rushed by, bringing many and varied experiences. In our vows, we made serious and sacred commitments to one other person exclusively, promising before God and those assembled that we would keep those vows for a lifetime. God enabled us to do this, and for that we thank Him with our hearts.

Forty-Fifth Anniversary
June 2, 1998

And now five years and forty have sped past
With mem'ries scattered like Fall leaves around;
Our children three have found true love and wed
To bring forth children that adorn our lives -
Eleven all together, babes to teens,
To bring us love and laughter in our hearts.
We've gone through fiery trials, shed bitter tears,
Have passed through pleasant meadows filled with peace.
We've lived in many places not our own
And after thirty years put down our roots.
We've traveled far and wide by car and train,
By helicopter, freighter, private plane;
Have seen our native land from sea to sea;
Have lived in cold and heat, have shivered, burned
'Neath sunny skies, in bush and city streets.

When first we met, we passed in busy halls
Where college classes tested our resolve
To graduate and then move on to missions.
(We didn't know each other at the time.)
But each of us had one high goal in common -
To set our feet one day on Afric's shore.
With this one common goal, our separate lives
Began to come together, bound with love.
It wasn't long till each of us discovered
That both of us could better reach the goal
If we were linked in marriage - man and wife -
Determined to serve Him in Africa.
And so we joined our hearts and hands, our lives,
Our goals, our dreams in 1953.
In course of time, God led us to the land
To which He called us, there to reach the lost.
We've lived in village distant, huge Accra,
Met with humble farmers, college students;
Shared their troubles, some of their diseases,
Had the joy of seeing dark lives changed.

We were tempered there and tried as gold,
Knew both joy and sorrow with our kids.
Called on God for grace when Death seemed near;
Learned to leave them, trusting, at His feet.
Sending them away was sacrifice,
Oftentimes, we said "Good-bye" with tears.
But He covered them with His great love,
And brought to each of them a Christian mate.

In time, He brought us back to Washington
To plant an inner-city Beacon church,
We saw a different life from that we knew
In far-off Africa where we had served.
The people were so different, hurt by drugs,
Domestic violence, and alcohol.
We found it hard to minister to such
And often longed for Africa once more.
Still, God had led us also to this work.
For twelve full years we gave it all our strength,
Leaned hard on Him and fellow-laborers
Until a church established stood alone.

Retired? No, we jumped into a role
Much different from the others we had known,
Not lowly farmers now, nor students keen,
Not inner-city folk with trials sore;
But the elderly, the lonely and the weak,
The faint of heart, the ailing and depressed.
He sent us, them to comfort and to sing
Sweet songs of trust and love for them to hear.

But through it all, two people joined as one,
Still serving Him together, still in love,
Still thanking Him Who brought us to each other
To have and hold, to cherish and to love.

78

Africa

While studying my missions course in college, I wanted desperately to go to Africa. Spending hours in a classroom and working long hours in a hospital did not satisfy my longing to GO somewhere and DO something for the Lord. But He assured me that I was where He wanted me to be and doing what He wanted me to do at that moment.

I Hear a Cry
December, 1951

Across the mighty ocean deep, dark Africa I see,
And lo! a burden on my heart arises suddenly.

I hear the lonely natives cry, their blinded eyes behold,
And long to see them rest for aye in Christ, the Shepherd's
fold.

Along the shore, in jungle dark, through desert scorched
and bare,
The need comes forth for witnesses the love of God to
share.

My feet would go today, O Lord, my hands would ready
be;
My tongue is here for Thy blessed use; I'd go - and
willingly!

But - Thou hast first a task for me which only can be
wrought
In preparation for Thy work, applying what is taught.

For witness here we must, before the Lord can send us
out
To give the Word to many lands, at home and all about.

So fill me, use me make me Thine; prepare me in Thy
will
That I may go to Africa, that needy place to fill.

Ken and I spent our first eight years in Wa, five-hundred miles south of the Sahara. Each December, the Harmattan winds began to blow down from the desert. No rain fell. Daily the skies, hazy with dust, showed brassy and the light of the sun was lessened. The wind blew incessantly, producing desert heat. It died down at night, bringing in desert cold. Everything dried up, including our stamps, shoes, photos and skin. But in the cold clear nights, the stars almost seemed near enough to pluck from the sky. At Christmas time, Ken took the children out to cut down an acacia tree for a Christmas tree, I baked cookies and we sang Christmas carols to some of the town principals such as the government agent, the doctor and the schoolmaster Gift-giving was simple. The turkey we had fattened for two weeks with corn was duly slaughtered and roasted. Just the smell of burning grass, the night chill and the change of season from wet to dry invoked cherished memories of Christmases gone by. Most importantly, we celebrated His coming.

Subsahara Christmas

It's Christmas again in Wa.
Overhead, the brazen sky throws oppressive heat
Upon us.
Even the birds lose some of their song
And the grass is parched and brown.
But in the velvet of the night
The stars shine -
Sparkling, twinkling radiant stars -
Each one of them with its own name.

Once upon such a shimmering night
Shepherds with their dumb charges
Stood overlooking Bethlehem town.
Startled they were by an Angel
Telling of Him.
Down from the stars moved the heavenly host
Radiant from being with Him.
Forth from their throats came the Heavenly song, "He is
born!"

It's Christmas again in Wa.
Forgetting the barren earth
Deprived of its fruit and dry,
We look up to our Savior
Rejoicing - He is born!

83

One of the unpleasant but necessary tasks of a new missionary is the discipline of learning the local language. In our case, we set up a table underneath the flamboyant tree and there, with an informant, we attempted to learn the Waalii equivalents of English words and expressions. Of course, similarities exist, but proverbs and idioms are much different and often difficult to understand even when translated. Two or three times a week I went to the home of Ajua, a Waala woman, to hear folk tales in the tribal language. At first, I could hardly follow the gist of the story. But as I heard it, it began to make sense. Later, when Ajua's precious baby died of malaria, I was able to comfort her in her own language. I wrote this for a new missionary, Nancy, many years ago. She now not only speaks the language but heads up a literacy program.

Language -The Shrine of a People's Soul

A woman will never empty her heart
Of the burden that's troubling her,
To the one who has come to her home and her side
For a witness of comfort and prayer,
If the visitor knows not the shrine of her soul -
The language she learned when so small;
For the secrets that lie in the depths of our breast
Are not easily brought through that wall.
Are you weary of grammar and sounds that are strange,
And you think that it matters not much?
Change your mind, my young friend; stay with the hard task,
If the soul of that one you would touch.

85

Inspirational

At one period in my life, I fled to Him and cried out for forgiveness. Engaged in a fierce battle with self, I felt I was losing. The sweet assurance I received soothed my troubled heart and brought healing. I rose from my knees glad and free!

Fallen - Forgiven

How can I, Father, again come to Thee
Seeking forgiveness so full and so free?
Sinful before Thee my heart trembling lies;
Help me, O Savior, and list to my cries.
Is there forgiveness? O, how can I pray
When Thou hast dealt patiently day after day.
Ask Thee for mercy when guilt bows me low?
My only refuge - to Thee I *must* go.
Can it be true that the blood covers all?
Can I assuredly rise from my fall?
Can I once more feel Thy peace in my soul?
Can I rejoice that the Lord makes me whole?

Cleanse me, Lord Jesus, O cleanse me until
Bowed in submission I bend to Thy will.
Sorry enough to forsake all my sin,
Willing to come and be cleansed all within,
Yielded as never before unto Thee.
Lord - cleanse my heart. Help me glorify Thee!

While working in the African bush large village of Wa, a very dear missionary friend discovered a lump in her breast. This necessitated a trip to Tamale, 200 miles away, for diagnosis and biopsy by a qualified surgeon. Of course the questions arose. What does this mean? The end of my missionary career? The beginning of the end of life? A mutilating surgery? Miserable chemotherapy? Pain? Packing up and returning to the States? No immediate answers came. She drove the distance alone on the dusty dirt roads, the tropical sun beating down on her car. Traveling on trust, she knew great relief to hear that the lump was benign and required no further treatment. Somehow, the trip back to Wa seemed shorter and easier than the one to Tamale. I wrote this for her. She still ministers with joy and blesses many other lives besides ours.

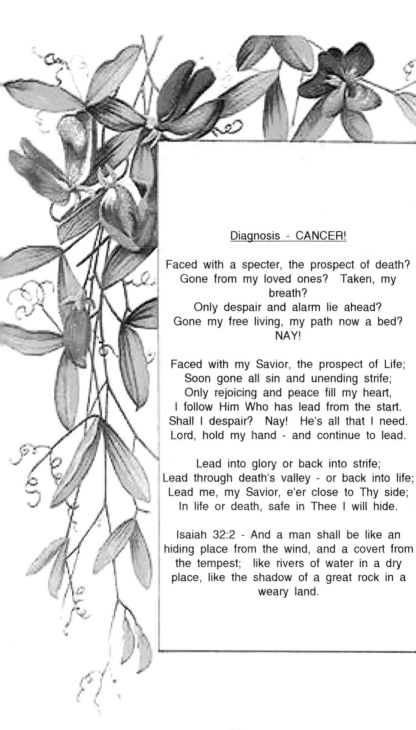

Diagnosis - CANCER!

Faced with a specter, the prospect of death?
Gone from my loved ones?   Taken, my
breath?
Only despair and alarm lie ahead?
Gone my free living, my path now a bed?
NAY!

Faced with my Savior, the prospect of Life;
Soon gone all sin and unending strife;
Only rejoicing and peace fill my heart,
I follow Him Who has lead from the start.
Shall I despair?   Nay!   He's all that I need.
Lord, hold my hand - and continue to lead.

Lead into glory or back into strife;
Lead through death's valley - or back into life;
Lead me, my Savior, e'er close to Thy side;
In life or death, safe in Thee I will hide.

Isaiah 32:2 - And a man shall be like an
hiding place from the wind, and a covert from
the tempest;   like rivers of water in a dry
place, like the shadow of a great rock in a
weary land.

Ken's beloved sister taught a class for adult women in her church. Once, as we visited her, she asked me to write a poem for them, concerning the peace that God can give a woman. This was for Barbara, now with Christ.

The Woman of Peace

Show me a woman with peace in her heart
And I'll tell you what you will find;
A joy to the downcast, a rest to the sick,
And one in control of her mind.

Her children she counsels, and God makes her
wise;
Her neighbors partake of her calm;

In sickness or trouble, she still remains cool,
Her own soul is soothed by that balm.

Her husband comes home from the work-a-day
world
All tired and worn and uptight.
He finds in his wife sweet peace and a smile
That somehow puts all the world right.

In church she's no gossip, she's really a friend
Who covers all faults with her love.
She's steady, she's helpful, she's humble and
sweet,
She does no more harm than a dove.

She's a wonder today in this maddening age
When hurry and worry prevail;
And the peace from Her Master that reigns in her
heart
Comes from a Source that can't fail.

As new missionary appointees, we attended a candidate seminar. We learned about some of the pitfalls awaiting us, including language and culture barriers, absence from family and friends, and difficult climate, as well as exposure to diseases we had only read about in medical books. One of the dangers was depression, very common when triggered by any or all of the above. "Prepare yourselves," we were told. "If it doesn't come in your first term, it will hit you in your second." Sure enough, Ken descended in the darkness within six months of our arrival. God delivered him through reading Psalm 42:11. "Why art thou cast down, O my soul? and why art thou disquieted within me? Hope thou in God; for I shall yet praise Him, who is the health of my countenance, and my God." My time of trial came in our second term. I had two miscarriages. This, together with long days and high stress, infections, and questions about God's leading in our lives, caused a tailspin for me. Then I discovered the power of the Bible. Words from the Psalms corralled and controlled the dark thoughts. Before that, I always felt that I would not want to live without Jesus Christ. After that, I realized that I could not live without Him. He is my center, my circumference, my reason for being. I wrote this for a friend who walked that dark road and came out into the light.

Delivered

Bound in the darkened cell, fettered in chains,
Captive to fears and held fast;
There was no way to escape from my pain.
I was a slave to my past.

Then, in the gloom, I perceived a small light
Piercing despair in my heart.
One ray of hope came into my dark cell,
Tearing depression apart.

Sun of my soul, God of my life,
I am now walking in light;
Praise fills my mouth, wonder my heart;
You are my song and delight.

Humbly I bow in Your presence now,
I am consumed by Your love.
Make me Your servant to live by Your Word
Till I am with you above.

One day, as I sat in the hospital cafeteria watching people, I was impressed with the fact that each of them hid true feelings behind a facade of calm. There were no sobs from those waiting for loved ones to become well or to die. Some who experienced deep sorrow from personal tragedies did not reflect that. Each was like someone in a house looking out their window eyes. God,
who knows our hearts, was aware of each one's feelings. He alone knew every person, every hurt and every hopeless heart. And His love reached out to them with compassion. "For God so loved the world, that He gave His only begotten Son, that whosoever believeth in Him should not perish, but have everlasting life"
John 3:16.

Observations

I see people in their "houses", looking out their "windows",
Hiding from intruders who would crowd them in their
spaces;
Guarded, wary, watching lest someone discover
What lies hidden deep within them.
So they spend a lifetime traveling as strangers,
Strangers in their houses as they look out through their
windows.

Andrew Murray's parents were British missionaries to South Africa in the nineteenth century. At the age of ten, he traveled to an English boarding school. He did not return to South Africa until he was twenty. Later, he ministered in a South African church. He also wrote many books of a devotional nature. These rules regarding behavior under trial have blessed me for years and I pass them down to others. The little poem, following the rules, sums up Murray's points.

Andrew Murray wrote this:

In times of testing say:

<u>First</u> - He brought me here, it is by His will I am in this place; in that I will rest.

<u>Next</u> - He will keep me here in His love and give me grace in this trial to behave as His child.

<u>Then</u> - He will make the trial a blessing, teaching me the lessons He intends for me to learn and working in me the grace He means to bestow.

<u>Last</u> - In His good time, He can bring me out again - how and when He knows.

So say, "I am here - by God's appointment, in His keeping, under His training, for His time."

This is my response:

<u>I Am Here</u>

I am here in this place for His time, by His grace
Learning much at His side. In this rock will I hide.
Though the storms rage around, safe in Him I'll be found
Drinking waters so still, for I'm kept in His will.

I knew Bud as a friend many years ago. Warmhearted and outgoing, he won the heart of seventeen year-old Irene. Later they began a marriage of more than thirty seven years. He always encouraged us, inviting us to spend time with them whenever we came to Tacoma. A teacher of English at a local high school, he also wrote poetry.

In his later years, he contracted cancer, but bravely fought the battle. We spent time with him and Irene on various occasions. One unforgettable scene occurred at Christmas Our family went to their home to sing carols. A few months away from death, Bud was dressed up in a bright red sweatsuit, wearing a broad smile as he listened to us sing. Though he knew his condition was terminal, he hired gardeners to develop his small Northwest garden, planting Oregon grapes, salal, and maple vines. My own little Northwest corner reminds me of him. The young marine kept his courage to the end of his life.

To My Friend - with Cancer

It takes a man of courage to climb a cliff's rock face;
A fingerhold or toehold help him to keep his place.

It takes a man of courage to face an angry beast;
He'd like to run away or hide, to say the very least!

It takes a man of courage to breast the current swift;
He struggles just to keep afloat - he dare not, MUST NOT
drift.

It takes a man of courage to face the journey's end
And stand down by the river beside his Unseen Friend.

It takes a man of courage to keep up with the fight;
To plant salal and maple vines and summon strength to
write.

You are that man of courage, Bud. You've shown us all
the way
To face the future bravely by living for each day.

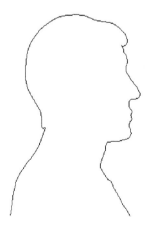

Bob and Alice Hayes were experienced Ghana missionaries whom we met in Kansas as new appointees in 1955. On their way back for their second term, they stopped by to see us and our brand-new firstborn in Johnson City, New York They met us in Accra when we arrived for our first term. Alice accompanied us to the Northern village of Wa, introducing us to the length of Ghana, from the capital city, through the Ashanti rain forest, up into the savanna hinterland. We expressed delight and amazement at clouds of butterflies we drove through. Crossing a river on a man-powered ferry, we resumed our journey on *corduroy - like* roads covered with red dust. When we lived in Tumu, we grew to love the Hayes family, the only other missionaries on the station. In August of 1998, Bob, now in another ministry, flew to Ghana for special meetings in the village of Techiman. There, his son John and daughter Sarah were working to open a new station. On their way back to the capital for Bob's return flight to the States, they had a head-on collision and all three were killed. John's wife was left a widow with three children. My beloved friend, Alice, lost her mate and both children. When I called her with tears, she said quietly, "Arlene, isn't God good?" Only someone who walks close to Him for a lifetime can say that at such a time. I sat in my living room trying to imagine what she was going through and wrote this.

For Alice Hayes

I've never felt my heart so sorely tried,
I never knew that it could hurt so much;
I sorrow sore e'en though my tears are dried,
I'm longing for my loved one's tender touch.
I try to face unnumbered comforters
With faith and calm (although my mind is numb);
I hear trite phrases, listen to kind friends,
But find no words to answer - I am dumb.

Oh, Suffering Savior, You alone I crave,
And You alone can fully understand
The pain that comes from sparing not a Son.
I kneel before You, reaching for Your hand.
I feel the presence of the Comforter
Whom You have left behind to succor me;
We ALL are Yours, my husband, daughter, son -
In this great grief, I'm clinging now to Thee.

In 1997 I attended a work retreat in an idyllic setting off the coast of British Columbia called Bowen Island. Our generous hostess, Barbie, assigned me a large bedroom with a huge plate glass window overlooking a cove. During the night when I woke up, I could see lights clear across the cove, but when dawn arrived, the morning mists crept in, obscuring the distant scene. It fascinated me and inspired me to write this poem. Thank you, Barbie.

Snug Cove

My life is a dinghy in Snug Cove - snug because I am in a safe haven and anchored to the Rock, Christ Jesus.

Sometimes, I am surrounded by moments of mist when I cannot see clearly or make either firm decisions or commitments. I need time and His direction.

At other times, lights across the cove show bright and distinct. I know where to go, what to do, how to respond.

My little craft in some seasons is jarred by angry gray waves with whitecaps. Tossed to and fro, rocking from side to side, dangerously near to capsizing, I cling to the Anchor that connects me to the unshakable Rock. I hold steady, and the dark forces assailing me pull back, defeated. I rest in calm seas.

Even in one given day -an ordinary, business-as-usual day - my moods can range from fearful to delighted, bemused, or angry and I need His assurance, reminding me that He loves, He cares, He controls. In Him, I can be steadfast, immovable always abounding in a life of joy.

Blessed Rock, may I continue to feel the tug of the anchor rope that holds me securely in Snug Cove. I would not want my life to end as driftwood, abandoned, thrown onto the beach as flotsam, of little use to anyone, heaped up helter-skelter in a pile of anonymity.

Many years ago, I meditated about the return of Christ to take His own back to the Home He has been preparing for them. The anticipation of this caused me great joy and I hurried to pin down the words as they came to my mind. "For the Lord, Himself shall descend from Heaven with a shout, with the voice of the archangel, and with the trump of God; and the dead in Christ shall rise first; then we which are alive and remain shall be caught up together with them in the clouds, to meet the Lord in the air; and so shall we ever be with the Lord. Wherefore, comfort one another with these words." 1 Thessalonians 4:16-18

Caught Up with Him

Caught up with Him! To leave it all behind us,
The sin that drags, the struggle to keep true,
The constant fight, the heartaches, disappointments,
To leave behind us - wondrous thought in view.

Caught up with Him! O blessed word of promise,
With clouds surrounded, He Himself appears.
He calls His own from grave, from plain, from city -
O blessed word - He beckons and we hear.

Caught up with him! Lord God, keep it before us
To make us pure and ready for our Home;
Help us to watch and listen for the trumpet.
He comes again! E'en so, Lord Jesus, come!